WILD and WOOLLY MAMMOTHS

by ALIKI

REVISED EDITION

HarperCollins*Publishers*

for G. Gregory Turak
and Nicholas Taylor Theodos

And for all my friends in Ohio—especially Maria Duttera,
Jacquelyn Hoover, Linda Woolard, Allan Pitcock, LeeAnn Lugar,
Rebecca and Lance Clarke, Sharon Low, Cleo Stoner, Bill Hughes
and Sue Grindrod. Thanks for the memories.

Mammoth appreciation to Joseph E. Wallace for his undaunted digging,
and to Virginia and Morton Sand for their impulse.

Library of Congress Cataloging-in-Publication Data   Aliki.   Wild and woolly mammoths / written and illustrated by Aliki.
p.   cm.   ISBN 0-06-026276-1. — ISBN 0-06-026277-X (lib. bdg.) — ISBN 0-06-446179-3 (pbk.)
1. Woolly mammoth—Juvenile literature.[1. Woolly mammoth. 2. Mammoths. 3. Prehistoric animals. 4. Paleontology.] I. Title.
QE882.P8A43 1996   94-48217   569'.6–dc20   CIP AC

Typography by Elynn Cohen   ❖   Revised Edition
Visit us on the World Wide Web!
http://www.harperchildrens.com

WILD and WOOLLY MAMMOTHS

4

A wild and woolly beast once roamed
the cold northern part of the earth.
It had two great, curved tusks
and a long, hairy trunk.
Its big bones were covered with tough skin
and an undercoat of soft, woolly fur.
Over that, its long shaggy coat of hair
reached almost to the ground.
It was an ancient kind of elephant
called a woolly mammoth.

Woolly mammoths flourished thousands of years ago.
Long, long before then, when dinosaurs lived,
the earth was hot and swampy.
But temperatures changed.
Parts of the earth grew cold.

In some places in the north, the snow never melted.
It froze over and formed thick sheets of ice called glaciers.
This was the time of the Ice Age.

Many animals died out because of the cold.
Other animals did not die out.
They migrated to warmer places and survived.
Still others remained in the cold north.
Every year, vast herds roamed across the icy plains
of Europe, Asia, and North America.

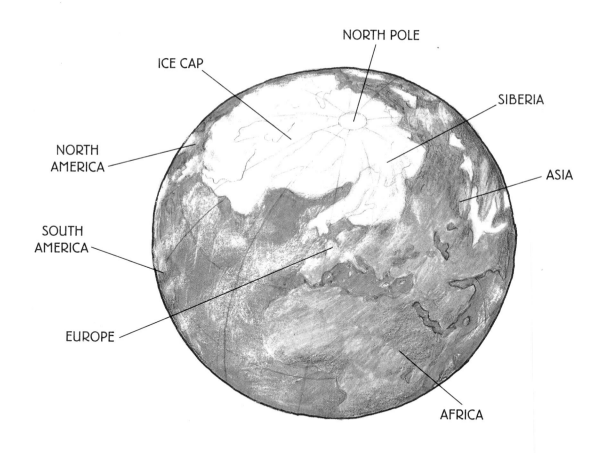

NORTH POLE

ICE CAP

SIBERIA

NORTH
AMERICA

ASIA

SOUTH
AMERICA

EUROPE

AFRICA

Only animals with heavy coats of hair, like the woolly mammoth, were able to survive the freezing cold. Their warm covering protected them.

GIANT ELK
(Megaloceros species)

WOOLLY RHINOCEROS
(Coelodonta antiquitatis)

MUSK OX
(Ovibos species)

BISON
(Bison species)

IBEX
(Capra species)

WOOLLY MAMMOTH
(Mammuthus primigenius)

These animals were also protected from the cold by fat. The woolly mammoth had a hump of fat on its back and head, and a three-inch layer of fat on its body.

It happened long ago
that one of these woolly mammoths
fell into a deep crack in a glacier.
It broke some of its bones and died.
Snow and ice covered its body.
The cold preserved its flesh.

Thirty-nine thousand years passed.
Slowly the weather grew warm again.
The thick layers of ice began to melt.
The Ice Age had ended.

In 1900, the mammoth's body was discovered in Siberia.
Part of it was poking out of the melting ice.
Travelers noticed their dogs sniffing the thawing meat.
The travelers did not know it was a mammoth, but it was.

Scientists uncovered the frozen body.

Only the exposed part had thawed and rotted.

The buried part was perfectly fresh—preserved by the ice.

Dogs ate some of the meat, and liked it,

even though it was thousands of years old.

Later, it is said, scientists tasted the mammoth flesh too,

and lived to brag about it.

The mammoth's last meal was still in its stomach.
It too was preserved by the cold.
And what a meal!
A mammoth thirty pounds of plant food.

A Mammoth's Diet

pinecones · pine needles · lichen · moss · twigs · grasses · ferns · flowers

More recently, scientists made another amazing discovery
in the stomach of a mastodon, a relative of the mammoths.
In the digested remains, they found live bacteria—
still preserved after 11,000 years.
The bacteria are the oldest living organisms ever found.

MAMMUT
Mastodon
found in Newark, Ohio, in 1989

Scientists found more woolly mammoths frozen in ice.
They found other kinds of mammoths, too, and studied them.
Now they know a great deal about these prehistoric animals.
"Mammoth" means giant, and they were.
Mammoths were the largest land mammals of their time.
They lived in various parts of the world, in diverse climates.

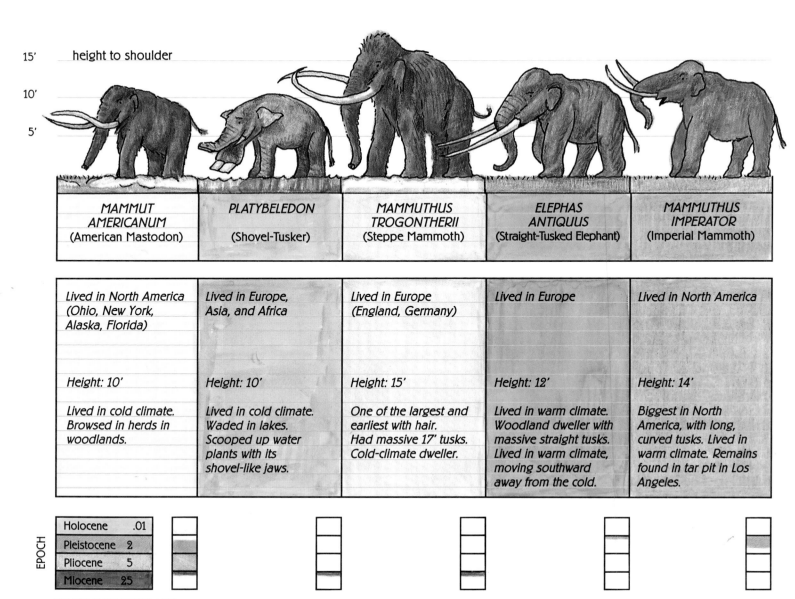

	MAMMUT AMERICANUM (American Mastodon)	PLATYBELEDON (Shovel-Tusker)	MAMMUTHUS TROGONTHERII (Steppe Mammoth)	ELEPHAS ANTIQUUS (Straight-Tusked Elephant)	MAMMUTHUS IMPERATOR (Imperial Mammoth)
	Lived in North America (Ohio, New York, Alaska, Florida)	Lived in Europe, Asia, and Africa	Lived in Europe (England, Germany)	Lived in Europe	Lived in North America
	Height: 10'	Height: 10'	Height: 15'	Height: 12'	Height: 14'
	Lived in cold climate. Browsed in herds in woodlands.	Lived in cold climate. Waded in lakes. Scooped up water plants with its shovel-like jaws.	One of the largest and earliest with hair. Had massive 17' tusks. Cold-climate dweller.	Lived in warm climate. Woodland dweller with massive straight tusks. Lived in warm climate, moving southward away from the cold.	Biggest in North America, with long, curved tusks. Lived in warm climate. Remains found in tar pit in Los Angeles.

EPOCH

Holocene	.01
Pleistocene	2
Pliocene	5
Miocene	25

MILLIONS OF YEARS AGO

Mammoths belonged to the Elephantidae family,
in an ancient group of Proboscidea—a group that includes
mammoths, mastodons, and modern elephants.
They are all animals with long trunks and tusks, hoofs,
and the flat teeth of plant eaters.
Today, only two species of elephants survive—those of Asia and Africa.
They are the last of the proboscideans, which first appeared
more than 50 million years ago.

15'   height to shoulder

10'

5'

ELEPHAS FALCONERI (Dwarf Mammoth)	MAMMUTHUS COLUMBI (Columbian Mammoth)	MAMMUTHUS PRIMIGENIUS (Woolly Mammoth)	ELEPHAS MAXIMUS (Modern Indian Elephant)	LOXODONTA AFRICANA (Modern African Elephant)
Lived on Mediterranean islands (Crete, Malta, Cypress, Sardinia)	Lived in southeastern North America (Carolinas, Georgia, Louisiana, Florida, California)	Lived in Europe, North America, Asia	Lives in Asia	Lives in Africa
Height: 3'	Height: 12'	Height: 9'	Height: 8–10'	Height: 13–14'
A dwarf island elephant. Lived in warm climate. Some island species survived for thousands of years after mainland species became extinct.	Had long, twisted tusks. Lived in warm climate in grasslands.	Shaggy, cold-climate tundra dweller. Hunted by early people. Not as big as some elephants, but powerful, and with a massive head.	Warm climate, feeds on leafy vegetation. Threatened by loss of habitat.	Lives in warm climate. Threatened by poachers, who kill it for its ivory tusks.

Mammoths traveled in peaceful herds.
In warmer seasons, they moved from grassy plains
to winding rivers, searching for food and water.
They shared their habitat with other plant eaters—
bison, horses, musk oxen, and caribou.
Sometimes they were attacked by smaller, fearless
carnivores—cats, wolves, or bears.
But there was one hunter even more dangerous
than the fierce saber-toothed cat, *Smilodon*.
That was the human hunter.

The mammoth hunters were cave dwellers.
They needed mammoths to live.
They hunted mammoths and other animals
with weapons they made of stone.
So their time is called the Stone Age.

Not long ago, remarkable wall paintings
were discovered in dark, damp caves.
They were made by Stone Age artists.
The paintings show the animals people hunted at that time—
mammoths, camels, bison, aurochs (ancient cattle), and horses.
Many of these animals are now extinct.
Artifacts, too, were found. They were carved in ivory,
bone, and stone, and tell about life long ago.

*Horse carved from
mammoth tusk
found in Germany*

*Bison and plants
carved in bone knife
found in France*

*Head carved in ivory
found in France*

More discoveries were made by archaeologists—
scientists who study ancient ruins.
They uncovered the remains of a whole Stone Age village.
They learned many things from this village and others like it.
They found out how mammoth hunters lived, and how
important the mammoth was to them.

In winter, clans lived in caves and in rock shelters,
protected from the cold.
In the spring, the snow began to melt.
The clans moved down to river valleys, where the
mammoths would come to graze.
Men, women, and children worked in groups.
They picked fresh grains, roots, grasses, herbs, and berries.
They collected bones of animals that the river washed down.
They used them to build elaborate shelters, covered
with mud and animal skins.
Then they prepared for the dangerous mammoth hunt.

21

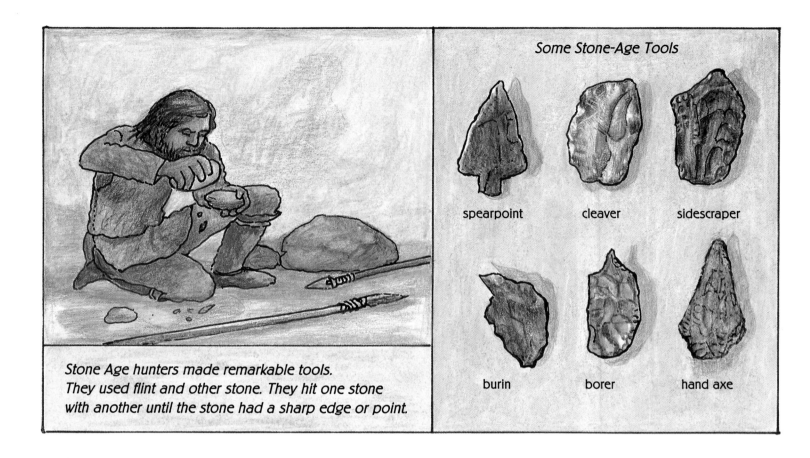

Some Stone-Age Tools

spearpoint   cleaver   sidescraper

burin   borer   hand axe

Stone Age hunters made remarkable tools.
They used flint and other stone. They hit one stone
with another until the stone had a sharp edge or point.

Toolmakers chipped knives, axes, and other tools
out of stone and mammoth bone.
They made razor-sharp spearpoints and attached
them to long, wooden spears.
With these, the hunters would kill the mammoths.
But first they had to find them and trap them.
Often they traveled far from their camps looking for them.

Sometimes the hunters set fires around the herds.
Then they forced the frightened beasts down steep cliffs.
Other hunters waited below to kill the mammoths with their spears.

Sometimes the mammoth
hunters dug deep pits.
They covered the pits with
branches, bones, and earth.

When a mammoth
walked over the pit,
the cover collapsed,
and the mammoth fell in.

It could not escape.
Hunters rolled heavy stones
down on the trapped mammoth
and killed it.

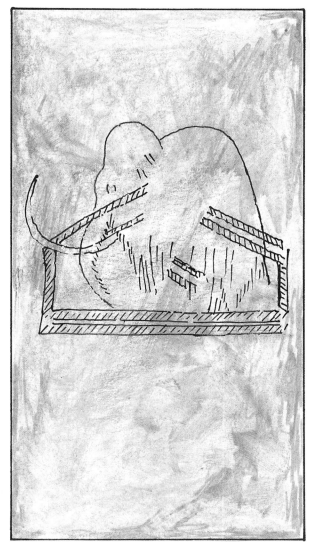

*Stone Age wall painting
found in a cave in France.
It shows a mammoth
caught in a pit trap.
Many mammoths that
were discovered showed
that their bones
had been broken,
and they had been
butchered with knives.*

Other animals were hunted for food and clothing too,
but a mammoth was a prized catch.
One was big enough to feed many people for a long time.
The group worked as a team to skin and butcher
the giant beast, and they saved nearly all its parts.
It was hard work.
They removed the brains and soft organs.
They cut and sliced the meat into pieces.
They removed the tusks, saved the fat and hide,
collected the bones.
They hauled it all back to their campsite.
Then they probably had a big celebration.

People used the skulls, tusks, and bones
for the foundations of their shelters.
It sometimes took the bones of 95 mammoths
to make one shelter.
They piled the bones around their camp, for ready use.

They used the mammoth's heavy hide as a door flap,
and cut it into strips for cords.
They twisted the long hair into cording for mats,
and used the woolly fur for bedding.
They burned bones for fuel.
They boiled the nourishing fat into a rich brew,
and used the fat for food, drink, medicine,
curing hides, and many other purposes.

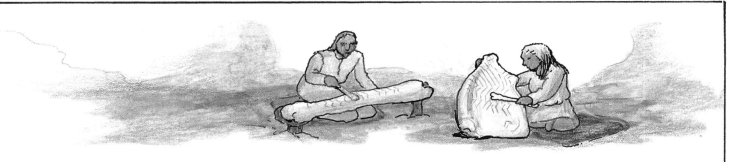

They made musical instruments out of the skull, bones, and tusks.
They used the stomach and intestines
as containers and cooking pots.
They carved the ivory tusks into jewelry, basins, utensils,
needles, buttons, ornaments, and sculptures.

They dried the fresh meat
to preserve it for winter.
They also stored and preserved
fresh meat in deep pits
they dug in the permafrost,
the permanently frozen ground
beneath the thawed, spongy soil.

Mammoth hide was too heavy to be used for clothing. Garments were made mostly of deer and bison skins and furs.

Season after season, herds of mammoths
continued to roam the tundras, steppes, and valleys
of the north.
Season after season, hungry cave dwellers
hunted them down.
This could be one reason why they died out.
No one is sure.